Amazing Jesus

Amazing *Jesus*

Dr Alastair T. Ferrie

iUniverse®

AMAZING JESUS

iUniverse books may be ordered through booksellers or by contacting:

iUniverse
1663 Liberty Drive
Bloomington, IN 47403
www.iuniverse.com
1-800-Authors (1-800-288-4677)

ISBN: 978-1-4917-6317-9 (sc)
ISBN: 978-1-4917-6318-6 (e)

Library of Congress Control Number: 2015904301

Print information available on the last page.

iUniverse rev. date: 03/25/2015

ACKNOWLEDGEMENTS

I gratefully acknowledge the help and encouragement of some close to me during the time that this book was being written. Some participated in proof reading the work for me and their helpful suggestions improved it greatly. In particular I would mention...

- Susan Dempsey.
- Bob Eckman.
- Linda Ferrie.
- Katheryn Haddad.
- John McCann
- Paula B.C. McDonald

and thank them for identifying examples of my ungrammatical style of writing. I tend to write as I preach and those who do both will know that you get away with some pretty ungrammatical sentence structures in public speaking which are not appropriate for the written word. As my doctoral supervisor put it with reference to my dissertation... "take this away and remove all the Alastairisms."

I am also grateful for the skill and dedication of those surgeons, doctors and nurses who cared for me in the past four years during some dark days. Ultimately I am thankful for the deliverance and grace of God who bestows such skill in human hands. But, most of all I am thankful for my wife Linda, without whose constant support and companionship I would not be able to write.

This book is written for those (identified in the spiritual growth studies written by the Willow Creek team as "Exploring Christianity") who are on the periphery of the church looking in, and considering Jesus and His claim on their hearts. To you this book is respectfully directed as we commend you for your interest in the Amazing Jesus of history and scripture.

Previous Publications:

Alastair Ferrie also has the following books in print:

Step-by-Step; Aftercare for New Christians (2004), published by iUniverse.

Evangelism in a Post Christian Culture (2008), published by iUniverse.

Seeing the Big Picture; A Christian's Guide to the Old Testament (2012), published by iUniverse.

All of the above are available from Amazon.com, Amazon.co.uk, iuniverse. com or good book shops everywhere.

Bible Quotations in this work are taken from a number of different translations, some old and some new. The following abbreviations are used to show which translation the quote is from:

BBE = BIBLE IN BASIC ENGLISH, PC Study Bible formatted electronic database Copyright ©2006 by Biblesoft, Inc.

ESV = ENGLISH STANDARD VERSION™, Copyright © 2000, 2001 by Crossway Bibles.

GNT = GOOD NEWS TRANSLATION - SECOND EDITION, TODAY'S ENGLISH VERSION, Copyright © 1992 American Bible Society.

NASB = THE NEW AMERICAN STANDARD BIBLE. Copyright © 1960, 1962, 1963, 1968, 1971, 1972, 1973, 1975, 1977, by The Lockman Foundation.

NASU = THE NEW AMERICAN STANDARD BIBLE UPDATE. Copyright © 1960, 1962, 1963, 1968, 1971, 1972, 1973, 1975, 1977, 1995, by The Lockman Foundation.

NCV = NEW CENTURY VERSION Copyright © 1987, 1988, 1991 by Word Publishing, a division of Thomas Nelson, Inc.

NKJV = THE NEW KING JAMES VERSION, Copyright © 1982, Thomas Nelson, Inc.

NLT = HOLY BIBLE, NEW LIVING TRANSLATION ®, Copyright © 1996, 2004 by Tyndale Charitable Trust.

NRSV = NEW REVISED STANDARD VERSION, Copyright © 1989, Division of Christian Education of the National Council of the Churches of Christ in the United States of America.

RSV = REVISED STANDARD VERSION OF THE BIBLE, Copyright © 1946, 1952, 1971 by the Division of Christian Education of the National Council of the Churches of Christ in the USA.

TEV = Today's English Version, First Edition, Copyright © 1976, American Bible Society.

TLB = THE LIVING BIBLE, Copyright © 1971. Tyndale House Publishers, Inc., Wheaton, IL 60189.

The Message = THE MESSAGE: The Bible in Contemporary Language, Copyright © 2002 by Eugene H. Peterson.

PROLOGUE

Bring Him your broken dreams, broken hearts, broken marriages, broken lives, and He can make all things well. When discussing the Christian life, it is all about a relationship with the Christ. Some two thousand years have passed since the days that Jesus walked this earth, and yet His influence seems as strong today as it was then, if not stronger. There are certainly many more who would acclaim Jesus as their king than anyone else in all history. His followers number in the billions. No one in all history has had the impact that Jesus of Nazareth has. He was a religious leader, philosopher. healer, miracle worker of all kinds. social reformer, teacher extraordinaire, preacher, instigator of behavioural transformation, King of kings and Lord of lords.

I have had a great privilege in life. I have been permitted to be a spokesperson for the King of kings and Lord of lords. I have spoken the word of hope concerning Jesus in many different locations. From the rural idyll of the Shetland Islands to the hustle bustle of London, England, the same message has gone forth and we have seen that message change the lives of men and women. In plush churches, and fancy halls I have stood and spoken of Jesus. In the homes of the poor and lowly I have sat in the quietness with people having no hope and no God, and told them the story of God's love and Jesus' sacrifice. I cannot begin to paint the picture of joy when baptizing those people into Christ, into family, and into hope. I wonder how many thousands of times I have told the story, and yet I am as thrilled with it today as I have ever been, in fact, more thrilled. I have lain in the cancer ward and looked around me at my fellow patients, facing up to one of life's greatest challenges, and wept for those with no faith. Some of my best writing was done in the day-room of the chemotherapy ward. Jesus has made the greatest difference in my life and He can make the same difference in yours. My hope is that every single person might receive the opportunity I received when I heard the gospel for the first time and rushed to embrace it.

I have conducted seminars in universities and spoken with those who were barely literate. Jesus loved every one, educated or non-educated, rich or poor, black or white. What is so amazing about Jesus?

He never wrote a book. He never travelled more than a few miles from His birthplace. He died young, not much more than thirty. On the day of His death, it looked like that would be the end of a great adventure. He had come, He had put forward a bold plan for a totally different kind of life and living. He revolutionised the thinking of His disciples, turning the world upside down with His teaching on love and selfless living. Now with His tragic and violent death, it seemed it was all over and everything would come to a halt. For the movement was all about Him. And with Jesus removed from the scene there did not seem to be much hope of such a movement continuing in any fashion.

Death Was Not the End.

Normally when a person dies, the impact that they made on the world begins to diminish and fade and a generation later there is very little left. Yet, this is not so with Jesus. His influence is greater than any other man who ever lived. Five hundred years after His death, the impact of Jesus on the world was infinitely greater than it was in His day. After one thousand years His legacy laid the foundations for the culture, learning and religion of much of Europe. After two thousand years He has more followers in more places than ever.

Rulers in history have often sought to be remembered by dating things according to the year of their reign in which a certain event happened. Or they have named cities after themselves (Alexandria, Caesarea etc.). All of these have been vain attempts at grasping on to eternity. Now we calculate all dating from one significant date in connection with the coming of Christ. The truth of the matter is that every time we consult our diary, or sign a cheque, we remember that all of our history is rooted in one truly magnificent historical Person and His coming into the world.

The Wow Factor:

It might be pertinent to ask why that should be. Why is it that Jesus of Nazareth has become the biggest icon in world history? He attracted such devotion that early Christians gave their lives willingly for Him, believing in His promise that they would be with Him in Paradise. And such is the strong magnetism of the Master that some even in the present day have been willing to pay the ultimate price for being a disciple also. What is there about Jesus that commands such devotion and loyalty? Ask any Christian and they will be quick to point out that their relationship with Christ is the most important relationship in their lives. There has to be a wow factor in that.

He taught people about human dignity, human worth, forgiveness, compassion and hope. He set forth a charter for His new kingdom—a fundamental value system that would determine the nature of that kingdom. And if you will let it, He would have it define your life too, so that you might have the marvellous blessings of living in the kingdom of God and bathed in the enlightenment which signals the abundant life of kingdom living. It is living in the light of God, in a world made dark by ignorance and confusion. He is indeed the Light of the World, calling us into His marvellous light.

His kingdom would be characterised by a couple of verses of Scripture that Jesus quoted. A smart-Alec lawyer had tried to trick Him one day by asking Him what the greatest commandment of the law was:

> *4 Attention, Israel!*
> *God, our God! God the one and only!*
> *5 Love God, your God, with your whole heart: love him with all that's in you, love him with all you've got!*
> *6 Write these commandments that I've given you today on your hearts. Get them inside of you 7 and then get them inside your children. Talk about them wherever you are, sitting at home or walking in the street; talk about them from the time you get up in the morning to when you fall into bed at night. 8 Tie them on your hands and foreheads as a reminder; 9 inscribe them on the doorposts of your homes and on your city gates. Deut 6:4-9 (THE MESSAGE.)*

This is the greatest commandment and another is like it, foundational in nature, revolutionary in purpose, transcendent and immutable as God Himself:

Lev 19:18

18 "Don't seek revenge or carry a grudge against any of your people. "Love your neighbour as yourself". I am God. (THE MESSAGE.)

Even before a word of the New Testament was written Jesus was in the business of expanding upon and reinterpreting the Old in favour of His new higher and better covenant, by which He would bring His people into the better promises of the eternal kingdom promised for ages past. The Jews had interpreted this statement as a command to love their fellow Israelites. Jesus in His new and better insight, reinterpreted this to be all inclusive. Even the Samaritan in the story of the Good Samaritan is given as a shining example of what this commandment should mean. The Jew was to love even the Samaritan. Black and white, slave and free, Rangers and Celtic, Protestant or Catholic, Muslim or Hindu, believer or pagan; none of this cancels out the deep inspiring commitment to love our neighbour. Indeed this is indicative of the revolutionary nature of the teaching of this Jesus of Nazareth.

Let me challenge you to read through this little book and ask you to examine the facts about Jesus of Nazareth. If perhaps these are things you heard before as a child, let me challenge you to re-examine them with adult eyes. Who knows? Perhaps this Jesus might end up amazing you too. It might turn out to be the most significant discovery of your life.

CHAPTER ONE

The Word Became Flesh

Each and every one of us needs to confront the essential truth about this Jesus of Nazareth. Who was He? What kind of man was He? Some say He was a prophet of God; one who came with a great message that would make mankind better and the world a better place in which to live. Some say He was a fraud, a trickster who cheated men and women into dying for Him. That would make Him some kind of megalomaniac, a madman who set Himself on a collision course with the authorities that inevitably resulted in His death. Perhaps He had a death wish. Was He the lunatic, the liar? Or was He the Lord? These are the choices we have to make.

In this short book, Bible references will frequently be mentioned, and I encourage you to read along from your own Bible.

Our beginning point is the majestic opening to John's gospel. It has often been commented that John's gospel is quite different from Matthew, Mark, and Luke. The emphasis is different; the purpose is different. Each of the four gospel accounts presents a different aspect of the overall picture of Jesus to us. Yet the four aspects are unique. The other three are similar in nature and are usually grouped together and referred to as the Synoptic Gospels, but John is different.

In Luke we have the historian's view, in Matthew the Jewish view, in Mark we have the Greek view but in John we have the view of the spiritual man. Here is the spiritual and eternal picture of Jesus. And in John we scale the heights, we fly with the eagle to catch a glimpse of the greatness of the One who came and who is Son of God. Now take time to read the first chapter of the gospel of John.

1

In the Beginning was the Word.

What is meant by the term, "beginning"? Clearly it refers to that which is before creation, since the work of the Word in creation is not referred to until v3. Before the world and time began, the Word (capital W) already existed.

This Word at a specific point in history became flesh (v 14) and lived among men in the person of Jesus Christ. This Word, though, pre-existed with God in eternity before the universe was created and before time began. Indeed everything that was created was created through Him. So a prime thought of this passage must be this: the Word is not one of the created things, He is the source of all creation.

The Word is not part of the world which came into being in time. The Word is part of eternity, there before time began, before the world was made, and the clock of the universe was set in motion. For God, the eternal One, the concept of time is not a limiting factor. It has no power to restrict the eternal nature of God. However, as soon as God began to make the temporal universe, then there was time.

This says something very important about the nature of God. Some think of a stern and bloodthirsty Old Testament God who began to look at things more lovingly through Jesus. But nothing could be further from the truth. If the Word was with God before time began, if the Word is part of the eternal scheme of things, it means that God was always like Jesus. Jesus is the embodiment of what God is. He is the very idea of God. Jesus is the exact representation of what God is like and what He has always been like. This concept is bound up in the use of this word Logos, Word of God. Jesus came to be the fullest revelation of the nature of God. God condescended to come in human form that we might see more clearly the nature of the One who seeks relationship with us. God was and is and always will be like Jesus, but man did not fully see it, or grasp it until God communicated it, by His Word. The Word of God is the ultimate communication of Godhood to man.

As we read through this first chapter of John there can be little doubt that the term "Word" is being used in some specialised way. We have only to notice v14 to see that the eternal Word became flesh and dwelt among us and we beheld His glory, glory as of the only Son from the Father.

Who can doubt that the main subject of this first chapter was the Son who came, Jesus?

But in this first chapter, a special title is given to Jesus, He is referred to as "The Word". The Greek term is "*logos*". It is really John's term. He introduces it and he uses it, and we have to conclude that it is the spiritual man John who discerns the Word of God. Note his use of the term also in the Revelation (*Rev 19:11-13*).

In the writings of John, this "denotes the essential Word of God, Jesus Christ, the personal wisdom and power in union with God, His minister in creation and government of the universe, the cause of all the world's life both physical and ethical, which for the procurement of man's salvation put on human nature in the person of Jesus the Messiah, the second person in the Godhead, and shone forth conspicuously from His words and deeds." (Thayer)

The Greek term means, (1) a thought or concept; (2) the expression or utterance of that thought.

As a designation of Christ, therefore, Logos is peculiarly apt because, (1) in Him are embodied all the treasures of the divine wisdom, the collective "thought" of God and, (2) He is from eternity, but especially in His incarnation, the utterance or expression of the Person, and "thought" of deity. In the Being, the Person, and the work of Christ, Deity is declared. Nothing declares God to humanity like the Word of God. Nothing communicates the depths of the infinite God to finite humanity like the Word of God.

The Word was *With* God!

What does that mean? Literally, it says that He was "*before the face of*". Does it simply mean that the Word could be found occasionally keeping company with God? Or is there some deeper significance and meaning to the phrase? Let us notice another statement later in the first chapter:

> *18 No one has ever seen God; the only Son, who is in the bosom of the Father, he has made him known. Jn 1:18. RSV*

Literally it says that the Word was "pros" = "with" God. One commentator says that this means in personal fellowship and closest

3

association. Another commentator says that it suggests the idea of being "face to face with God". There were other words that could have been used if the concept of "with" meant less than this. It means living relationship, intimate converse. It suggests the idea of presence and communion. In what sense was He with God?

1. **In relationship to time and eternity:** As God is Himself eternal and outside of the constricts of time, coming from eternity and inhabiting eternity and is Himself the author of time and creation, so also is the Word with God in these things.

2. **In His manner and mode of being:** The Word cannot be bracketed with man, nor anything else in all creation, for He is the agent of creation and outside of creation itself. Nothing was made without Him so it would be improper to class Him with creation. Clearly if He was the One who created and without Him was not anything made that was made, then He must be regarded as being associated with omnipotence. He is a Being who is nothing less than all powerful, and so with God in this matter.

3. **In nature and character:** The Word is one with God in nature and character. The Bible is replete with passages affirming this great truth. "If you have seen Me you have seen the Father," says Jesus. In the Hebrew epistle (Heb 1:3), it says that Jesus bears the very stamp of the nature of God. He is the perfect and faithful representation of what God is like. John, in the wonderful opening to his first epistle in the New Testament proclaims that they were eye witnesses. We saw Him, we heard Him, we touched Him. The eternal life which was "with" the Father has now been made manifest to us, His witnesses to the world (*1 John 1:1-4*).

The Word Was God.

Perhaps this statement is the most profound of all. This statement comes from the absolute heights of the eagle's flight. *And the Word was God.*

If there was any danger that anyone might misunderstand his previous statement about the Word being with God, John is going to expand upon it. It was not just that the Word was keeping company with God, the Word was God.

There can be little doubt that man has a philosophical difficulty with this. Yet it is there; it is an "in your face" kind of statement; there for us to grapple with. Perhaps we cannot understand it fully until we fly with the eagle to the highest heights of spiritual understanding and perception. Yet it is there. It is still true. The Word was God! No doubt, some Christians reading this will question the wisdom of my beginning with this thought. It is immense. It is the biggest thought of all. God became flesh.

> *5 Have this mind among yourselves, which is yours in Christ Jesus, 6 who, though he was in the form of God, did not count equality with God a thing to be grasped, 7 but emptied himself, taking the form of a servant, being born in the likeness of men. 8 And being found in human form he humbled himself and became obedient unto death, even death on a cross. 9 Therefore God has highly exalted him and bestowed on him the name which is above every name, 10 that at the name of Jesus every knee should bow, in heaven and on earth and under the earth, 11 and every tongue confess that Jesus Christ is Lord, to the glory of God the Father. Phil 2:5-11 RSV*

He was in the form of God. When? In the beginning. Where? In heaven.

The Greek for God is *"theos"*. And the definite article "the" in the Greek is "ho". Now the Greeks when they used a noun almost always use the word "the" with it. When the Greek speaks about God, it does not simply say "theos", it says "ho theos." When the Greek does not use the definite article it means that the noun becomes not so much a noun and a bit more like an adjective; it describes the character, the quality of the object in question.

But it is interesting that John did not write that "the Word was the God". He did not say that the Word was *"ho theos"*. That would have been to say that the Word was identical with God. He says that "God was the Word". Theos—without the definite article. This means that the Word was, as we might say, of the very same character and quality and essence and Being as God.

Some in their desperation to sustain an unbiblical concept have been unhappy with this translation and have produced their own translation (e.g. The New World Translation or NWT) in which they say the Word was "a" God, whatever that means. But it is not a required translation at all. Indeed in the New World Translation we find that, although the same construction is used in v18, the NWT does not insert the word "a" in that verse.

Barclay says of this verse: *"Jesus is so perfectly the same as God in mind, in heart, in being that in Jesus we see perfectly what God is (like)."*

A Parable.

Bear with me in a little foolishness as I tell you a parable. As you know a parable is a story that can be understood on more than one level. It makes some degree of sense in the most straightforward understanding, but there is an underlying message which is spiritually and eternally true.

There was a man who spent his whole life studying the Auchenshuggle Dung Beetle. He knew everything there was to know about this creature, and he had several friends who were similarly enthralled with the scientific study of its life cycle. However all the scientists came to the same conclusion that the beetle had developed certain lifestyles which were destructive and the whole species was in danger of going out of existence. They held an emergency meeting. What could be done? How do you teach a dung beetle a different way of life and so preserve its existence? As the scientists discussed this one suggested that the only way to really communicate with those creatures would be if a dung beetle could communicate with its own kind and show them the way to survive, to be saved from their own self-destructive tendencies.

Another of them pointed out that he had just invented a machine that could change a creature's DNA structure and theoretically, could take a human being and turn him into a dung beetle. There was a sudden quiet around the room. Who would care enough to make that kind of sacrifice? Who would become a dung beetle to save dung beetles?

The story of the gospel says that Jesus would. He became a human being to save human beings. God became a man, for you and me.

Conclusion:

Let us conclude by simply reading some passages of Scripture together:

> *₁ God, who at various times and in various ways spoke in time past to the fathers by the prophets, ₂ has in these last days spoken to us by His Son, whom He has appointed heir of all things, through whom also He made the worlds; ₃ who being the brightness of His glory and the express image of His person, and upholding all things by the word of His power, when He had by Himself purged our sins, sat down at the right hand of the Majesty on high, Heb 1:1-3 NKJV*

> *In the beginning was the Word, and the Word was with God, and the Word was God. ₂ He was in the beginning with God. ₃All things came into being through him, and without him not one thing came into being. What has come into being ₄ in him was life, and the life was the light of all people. ₅ The light shines in the darkness, and the darkness did not overcome it. John 1:1-5 NRSV*

> *₁₈No one has ever seen God. It is God the only Son, who is close to the Father's heart, who has made him known. John 1:18 NRSV*

> *₂₈ Thomas answered him, "My Lord and my God!" ₂₉ Jesus said to him, "Have you believed because you have seen me? Blessed are those who have not seen and yet have come to believe." John 20:28-29 NRSV*

> *₁₁ For the grace of God has appeared, bringing salvation to all, ₁₂ training us to renounce impiety and worldly passions, and in the present age to live lives that are self-controlled, upright, and godly, ₁₃ while we wait for the blessed hope and*

the manifestation of the glory of our great God and Saviour, Jesus Christ. ₁₄He it is who gave himself for us that he might redeem us from all iniquity and purify for himself a people of his own who are zealous for good deeds. Titus 2:11-14 NRSV

₈But of the Son he says, "Thy throne, O God, is for ever and ever, the righteous sceptre is the sceptre of thy kingdom. Heb 1:8 RSV

I, Simon Peter, am a servant and apostle of Jesus Christ. I write this to you whose experience with God is as life-changing as ours, all due to our God's straight dealing and the intervention of our God and Saviour, Jesus Christ. 2 Peter 1:1-2 (from THE MESSAGE)

₂₀And we know that the Son of God has come and has given us understanding, to know him who is true; and we are in him who is true, in his Son Jesus Christ. This is the true God and eternal life. 1 Jn 5:20 RSV

Nothing declares deity like the Word of God, who became flesh and in so doing was the finest declaration of deity and highest potential of humanity simultaneously. God became flesh and dwelt among us.

Hey! What's the big idea? There is none bigger than this. God came down to be near us. He came to dwell among us. He came in order to reveal Himself fully, that we may see Him and come to know Him and come to have a close personal relationship with Him.

The Apostle John thinks that this is the logical place to begin, and so begins his story here. Christ in eternity before the world was framed, before time began. In a sense, it makes the rest of the story logical. We could not say that one day God came to earth and nothing out of the ordinary happened. This would be totally unbelievable. God came down; a virgin gave birth to a baby boy. God came down, and miracle after miracle was performed before countless witnesses. God came down, and man treated Him shamefully and tortured Him to death on a Roman cross, but the grave could not hold Him and He arose on the third day and appeared to many witnesses, who were prepared to die rather than change that testimony. That the Word who was God, became flesh and dwelt among us, full of the glory of His Heavenly Father, makes sense of the rest of the story.

CHAPTER TWO

Jesus: Miracle Man

Let me tell you something of the amazing story of amazing Jesus. When Jesus came to be with us on earth, wherever He went, miracles kept happening. What do we mean by miracles? One dictionary definition is, "an event or effect in the physical world deviating from the known laws of nature, or transcending our knowledge of these laws: a wonder or wonderful thing; a marvel." (Webster's New Collegiate Dictionary) C.S. Lewis defined a miracle as "an interference with Nature by supernatural power." The Westminster Dictionary of the Bible gives an even better definition: "Miracles are events in the external world, wrought by the immediate power of God and intended as a sign or attestation".

In John's gospel these miracles are referred to as signs. This again emphasizes that they had a purpose. They are not just wondrous events, worthy of discussion. They are meant to signify something. They are signs pointing toward something; in this case the deity of the Christ.

Some people of course have problems with the miracles. They do not want to accept that such things happened in biblical times. But these problems stem from a weak view of God and His Son Jesus. The real problem then is not with miracles, but with the whole concept of God. Once we are convinced about the existence of God then miracles are no problem. In fact it would be utterly astonishing if they did not exist. The converse is also true... if we are convinced about miracles, then the existence of God is a given. These miracles of Jesus after all were demonstrably not mere confidence tricks or psychological tricks, but limbs grew back, congenital conditions were corrected, the blind saw for the first time, the deaf heard, the dead raised.

The miracles of Jesus were never performed for personal prestige or to gain money or power. They were always performed for the benefit of others and for the highest motivations. Jesus Himself saw them as of paramount importance in declaring His deity to the world, as He told the Jewish leaders of His day, the works that I do, they bear witness to me (*Jn 10:25*). "Believe me for the sake of the works themselves", challenges Jesus. (Jn 14:11)

The Nature of Christ's Miracles.

The miracles of Jesus were both frequent and varied. It was not the case that sometimes He could do miraculous things and sometimes He could not. There were never occasions when He set out to perform a miracle and had to give up because His magic wouldn't work.

Also it is notable that there was a tremendous variety to the miraculous things that Jesus could do. It was certainly not the case that the Lord had a few magic tricks up His sleeve and the five tricks were rotated as He performed them in different towns. There was a tremendous variety to the amazing signs which Jesus was able to perform at will.

Such miracles are usually classified into the following main groups:-

- Power over nature.
- Power over disease.
- Power over demons.
- Power over the material world.
- Power over death.

Power over nature.

On one occasion the disciples were crossing the Sea of Galilee in a boat when Jesus came to them walking upon the water. This displayed power over gravity, one of the most fundamental of the laws of Nature. Yet Jesus as Lord of this Creation displayed His mastery over it. He fed the five thousand, turned the water into wine, stilled the storm and did all manner of things that displayed His mastery over His creation.

Power over disease.

One accusation which has been made by many concerning the healing miracles is that they must have been chiefly over psychosomatic illnesses. Indeed much of the modern "faith healings" would appear to fall into this category. Can this be said of the healing miracles of Jesus? Lepers who had been diagnosed as suffering from the disease and banished to live outside society were instantly cured. There is nothing psychosomatic about leprosy. Yet they were cleansed at His command. They walked away and were healed as they walked. Psychosomatic? Never. Then there were clear-cut cases of healing congenital disease, such as the man born blind (John 9). This man's blindness wasn't something that had only just come upon him. He had been blind from birth. His family knew it, his neighbours knew it, the whole town knew it. Indeed this is commented in the chapter itself *(Jn 9:32-33)*.

But he went to the pool and came back seeing after meeting with Jesus. Another example of this most common type of miracle that Jesus performed is His healing of the servant of a centurion who lived in Capernaum. The narrative relates that on entering Capernaum, Jesus was met by a centurion whose servant was lying paralysed at home. Jesus immediately offered to go with the man to heal his servant. However in a defining moment of tremendous faith the man replied that Jesus would not even need to come, just speak the words and it shall be done *(Matt 8:5-11)*.

What was it that endeared Jesus to so many? What was it that gathered such crowds wherever He went? It was that His ability to heal diseases that no doctor could cure, and no medicine could help.

Power over demons.

It is difficult for us to tune into this kind of miracle when we have no personal experience of it. Most of us have encountered and even experienced ill health before, but when the Bible talks about Jesus casting out demons it is difficult for us to imagine this or picture it in our minds.

The account is given in Mark 5:1-13 of a wonderful event on the shores of the Sea of Galilee. Jesus is met by a man possessed by many demons. When I say, "met," you have to picture the scene. Jesus has just gotten out of the boat with His disciples when a naked wailing banshee of a figure comes running at them from the tombs. He is covered with cuts and bruises. His body is a mess and his unkempt appearance adds to the terrifying nature of this encounter. If I had been one of the disciples of Jesus, I would have been first back in the boat and first to cast off. Here is a man so deeply troubled that no one would pass that way in case they met him. They had tried tying him up, and binding him even with chains. However in every case he tore the bonds apart with his bare hands. The Lord speaks gently to the man commanding the legion of unclean spirits to come out of him. At the request of the demons themselves, Jesus cast them into a great herd of pigs and they all ran headlong into the sea and were drowned. The forces of evil are always destructive. When the people of the district came out to see what had been going on, they found the man fully clothed, and in his right mind (*Mark 5:1-13*).

What are we to make of this demon possession business? We may never have experienced it in this day and age. Yet,

- in the ministry of Jesus it was commonplace to find demon possession...
- and in the ministry of the apostles following, it was present if not as common,
- and we notice that in the writings of the epistles it seems to disappear from the story.

Many scholars believe that the prevalence of demon possession at the time of the ministry of Jesus and the beginning of the church is compelling evidence of the opposition of the devil to the setting up of God's kingdom. When in due season the kingdom was established, we see their interference diminish as Satan saw that the Spirit had been bestowed and his efforts were fruitless. Demons almost certainly do not act in the same way today. God would not permit anyone or anything to so take control of us that we were not responsible for our own actions or choices any longer. With every temptation, the Lord always provides a way of escape. But nevertheless such demons were very active in the time of Christ and He exhibited absolute authority over them. And if we are tempted to doubt the existence of demons in the time of Christ, then we have to remember that the existence of evil in the world, the existence of Satan as the orchestrator of all evil, and hence the existence of demons—the angels of evil, are intuitively obvious.

Power over material things.

Jesus showed His power over the material universe in a number of ways. One example was when Jesus multiplied the five loaves and two fishes until there was enough food to feed five thousand men, besides women and children (Matt 14:13-21).

Another example would be turning water into wine at the wedding feast in Cana (See John ch 2).

Power over death.

Perhaps the most startling sign of all was the power displayed by Jesus over death itself. We know that on hearing of the illness of Lazarus His friend, Jesus delayed His journey to Bethany until after Lazarus had died. Even though Lazarus had been dead in the tomb four days, Jesus called him forth and he came walking from the tomb. See Jn 11:1-44.

This was the most dramatic and most undeniable instance of Jesus raising the dead. On two other occasions, it is recorded by the apostles and witnesses, Jesus raised the dead. He had raised the young daughter of Jairus (Mark 5:21-43) and the widow's son at Nain (Luke 7:11-17).

In those days burial took place on the day of death. In both of these cases Jesus raised the dead immediately after death and before burial had taken place. No doubt there would be some who would prefer to deny such a miracle and would say that the person was not dead but merely in a death-like coma. If this were to be the case then the Lord Jesus did not raise the dead but simply healed and roused two people from a death like coma and brought them to active life once more. Still pretty amazing. A miracle indeed!

However this charge cannot be made with reference to the raising of Lazarus. He had been dead in the tomb for four days. People travelled for miles to see the man who used to be dead. Many walked the short distance from Jerusalem (about two miles) to see dead Lazarus walk, speak, or eat. Largely this was the reason why a few days later thousands came out to welcome Jesus into Jerusalem as Messiah because He had raised the dead (Palm Sunday).

The Importance of the Miracles.

These miraculous signs were regarded by Jesus to be important. They were the means by which the validity of His ministry was demonstrated to the people. They were the means by which people would know that He had come from God and was the representation of God to the nation. "Believe me because of the works that I do", said Jesus.

We should recall the following points about these miracles.

First the miracles were done in public. They were not performed in secret before only one or two people who announced them to the world. Suppose all the miracles performed by Jesus had only ever been seen by Peter and John and we relied wholly on their testimony. We would expect the sceptics to have a field day with that. But they are validated on the basis of eye-witness testimony of many people. These things were not done in a corner, but in full view of the multitudes. Men who had been lame beggars all their lives, stood and leapt and ran. There was no argument. The man blind from birth, saw and walked home seeing. None could deny it. For this reason, the leaders of the Jews became very nervous about the growing influence of Jesus on their nation. Perhaps everyone will believe in him, and where will we be then? (*John 11:45-49*).

Second we note that when the opponents and enemies of Jesus wished to attack Him, they did not say that He never performed miracles. That was beyond question. What they said was that He must have done it by the power of the devil (*Matt 12:22-25*).

This showed that they could not attack the veracity of the signs themselves. It is one thing to ask people to believe in miracles because some people claim to have witnessed them. But it is quite another to have the concrete proof standing in front of you in the person of a blind man given sight, a leper cleansed, or a lame man who now leaps and runs.

Third, we note that some miracles were performed in the presence of unbelievers. It is notable that in modern times, events which are claimed as miracles are not performed in the presence of the sceptic. With Jesus, people were compelled to believe in Jesus against their will by the evidence of their own eyes and ears. It was not a requirement for Jesus that to witness one of his miracles you had to first of all be a believer. There was none of that nonsense with Jesus. Sceptic and believer alike were convinced that a miracle had taken place. They may disagree about the source of the power for it, but the fact of the miracle was not in dispute.

Fourth, we note that there was the unconquerable testimony of the cured. You may recall that the triumphal entry of Jesus into Jerusalem was that which triggered the final opposition of the Jewish leaders and resulted in His crucifixion. What was it that gathered such crowds to welcome Him and to acclaim Him as the promised Messiah? You will note that it followed a few days after the resurrection of Lazarus. To fulfil the prophecy concerning the triumphal entry was very simple; it only required to raise someone from the dead. His is the classic case of a healing which could never be explained away as being psychosomatic. In John ch 9 what could they do with the man born blind for his healing was undeniable and his testimony was plain:

> *24 So they sent a second time for the man who had been blind and they said to him, Give glory to God: it is clear to us that this man is a sinner. 25 He said in answer, I have no knowledge if he is a sinner or not, but one thing I am certain about; I was blind, and now I see. John 9:24-25 BBE*

The miracles of Jesus are integral to the story. You cannot go through the story of Jesus and seek to remove all that is miraculous from it... for you would destroy the message that God wants you to have. The miracles were an integral part of the ministry of Jesus, and all accepted that He performed such signs, both friend and foe alike.

When Nicodemus, who since he was one of the leaders of the Jews must be regarded as part of the opposition, came to Jesus by night, his conclusion should be noted: your must be from God, because no one could do the things that you do unless you were from God (*John 3:2*).

Nicodemus was right. He had come to faith because of the signs, because of the miracles which Jesus did.

In closing, consider the case of Judas Iscariot. He had made up his mind to betray Jesus. What could have been more damaging than to give the low down, give the first hand evidence of all the tricks that Jesus had been pulling to fool the people. On this score, the lips of Judas are sealed. He had nothing to say. All he can do is tell the Jews where Jesus prayed.

Seeing is Believing.

There are some who would say that Jesus should have come in our day and age. He would have been able to perform His miracles on satellite television to a world-wide audience and then everyone would believe in Him. If only that were true. There would be many who would view the miracle performed on their screen and still refuse to believe in Jesus. They would suggest it was a trick of the camera angle, or a fraud. The cameras were stopped and the baskets were filled up again and again so that the fishes and the loaves would go round the crowd. There were stepping stones in the sea and Jesus hopped from one to another, only the camera didn't show you that. Ridiculous suggestions such as this have been made down through the ages. There were some who were eye-witnesses of the miraculous powers of the Messiah but who refused to believe despite the evidence of their own eyes. We have the testimony of eye witnesses and some choose to believe that testimony whilst others thrust it from their minds. Some have seen yet do not believe. Some have not seen and yet believe. Hence perhaps the heading of this paragraph needs to be changed:

- *Believing is believing.*
- *Believing is a decision that we make based on the evidence we have been shown.*
- *Believing is a matter of choice.*
- *Hearts that are open to the love of God will "see" in Jesus the power of God and believe.*
- *Eye witness testimony is the basis on which every court in the land operates. Now what will we do with the eye witness testimony concerning Amazing Jesus.*

CHAPTER THREE

Healer of Body and Soul

I n the history of mankind, there never has been a healer like Jesus. When we think of the miraculous ministry of Jesus it is to healing miracles that our minds turn. It seems that everywhere we look in the New Testament we see a picture of the healing Jesus. It is perhaps the thing He is remembered for more than anything else. Let us remind ourselves of this compelling picture by reading Luke 17:11-19.

In this passage Jesus met ten men who were lepers. Leprosy meant that a man had to live outside communities, separated from his loved ones and family, whilst the disease ravaged his body. They cried out to Jesus for help. Their situation was hopeless. However, Jesus simply commanded them to go and show themselves to the priest for he had authority to allow them back into the midst of community and life. As they went, they were healed.

This incident is typical of so many recorded in the gospel records. Jesus is travelling along the road passing between Samaria and Galilee. Clearly He must have been in Judea in the south and travelling back up towards Capernaum and his base there from which He carried out His great Galilean ministry.

As He travels He meets ten unfortunate men. They are sufferers from one of the most deadly and crippling diseases known to ancient man. Sufferers had such little hope of any remission or cure. And as a sufferer of leprosy they would be condemned to live outside of normal society in order to protect society from a disease with no known cure and no effective treatment. They stand at a distance and cry out to Jesus for help. Even without touching the men, nor applying any medicinal treatment whatsoever, Jesus is at a word able to bring healing into their tragic lives. After being passed by the priests as being in remission they would be able to return home once more. They would be able to sleep and dwell in their own homes. They would go back to working for a living in the midst of society and be able to resume a normal life.

Although ten are healed, Jesus laments that only one of the ten thought to return and offer thanks for such transformative healing. This man was a Samaritan. Who is this Jesus that He can speak healing into existence, and the incurable suddenly becomes cured, and the hopelessness of the incurable are brought to hope and life. No wonder that marvelling Samaritan returned to offer thanks. The healing Jesus has brought new life into existence because of love. Even if some of these men were so preoccupied by the sudden hope springing up in their breast that they forgot to thank Him, later they would realize just how much the Lord had done for them in this selfless act.

As we turn to the gospel of John (see John 5:1-9), we recall that though the Lord performed thousands of miracles, here in this book, John, directed by the Holy Spirit, selects only seven of these miracles to record in his version of the story of Jesus. Only seven! But these seven are so special, so significant that John realises that in just relating these seven, there is enough evidence that we might fall in love with Him immediately and want to give our lives to Him forever.

Here is a man whose whole life was being swallowed up in illness and incapacity. Every day was a challenge. Every day there was pain and discomfort. Life consisted of being carried to the pool each day and lying by the pool hoping against hope that the superstition of the people might be true. They believed that the days in which the pool was troubled by the flow of the stream coming through Hezekiah's tunnel might result in his being first into the pool and an inexplicable and unexpected healing.

Jesus came to the man and asked him a question. "Do you want to be healed?" This may seem like an unusual question. What a question to ask. Yet it is a question which is a reasonable one for if the man has learned to accept his disability and no longer hopes to be free of it then perhaps he would not accept the healing that Jesus had to offer. The more we contemplate the spiritual significance of this healing, the more we see that there are times when we are crippled by sin and no longer wish to be free. But Jesus asks this question to the suffering man, "Do you want to be healed? Stand up and walk". How much faith was involved in that first attempt to stand on unsteady feet? Then tentatively, to take those first steps, and later to run and jump for the sheer joy of being able to do so. He arose, picked up his rolled up pallet on which he spent his whole life and walked for the first time in thirty-eight years. Disability was replaced by joyful capacity, to walk and run and jump and rejoice.

Oh what a transformation from the lips of a healing Jesus. Wherever the master went, healing went with Him.

> *35 While He was still speaking, some came from the ruler of the synagogue's house who said, "Your daughter is dead. Why trouble the Teacher any further?" 36 As soon as Jesus heard the word that was spoken, He said to the ruler of the synagogue, "Do not be afraid; only believe." 37 And He permitted no one to follow Him except Peter, James, and John the brother of James. 38 Then He came to the house of the ruler of the synagogue, and saw a tumult and those who wept and wailed loudly. 39 When He came in, He said to them, "Why make this commotion and weep? The child is not dead, but sleeping."*

> *40 And they ridiculed Him. But when He had put them all outside, He took the father and the mother of the child, and those who were with Him, and entered where the child was lying. 41 Then He took the child by the hand, and said to her, "Talitha, cumi," which is translated, "Little girl, I say to you, arise." 42 Immediately the girl arose and walked, for she was twelve years of age. And they were overcome with great amazement. 43 But He commanded them strictly that no one should know it, and said that something should be given her to eat. Mark 5:35-43 NKJV*

Every death is a sad affair. When we hear of some great of the faith who has served the Lord faithfully all of their days, our sadness is reduced somewhat by the assurance of a great reward awaiting that loved one and a regal welcome as one who is welcomed home after a successful battle and a victorious campaign.

But the death of a young person is always a matter of great sorrow. It seems unnatural; unfair somehow. Hers was a life full of promise and potential brought to an end suddenly before its time. How often there are feelings of great distress over this kind of death. And yet of course the Lord offers comfort as only He could in these circumstances, if we have eyes of faith to see it.

In this incident recorded in Mark's gospel, Jesus is called to the house of an important man, a ruler in Israel. But that house has been struck with tragedy. The daughter of Jairus, a mere 12 years of age, who was suffering and desperately ill had died, even whilst the Master was en route to help her. How tragic is that? So near and yet so far. Just as the first rays of hope bore softly like the dawn of a new day, it seemed to reverse by a plunging into darkness like an unwelcome eclipse. The cold and terrifying news of death came. When the Master arrived at the door the sound of weeping was almost overpowering. The child is dead. You need not come any further.

- **All of their hopes had been dashed.**
- **All of their prayers had been for naught.**
- **All of their efforts to find Jesus and bring Him there before death should strike... have been for nothing.**
- **There is nothing left but to mourn.**
- **And every day they would regret and mourn the loss of one so loved and so young.**

Jesus had an inner group of three disciples (Peter, James and John) within the twelve, and on certain occasions we see Jesus selecting them to be taken somewhere with Him at special times of service, concern, prayer, or difficulty (the Mount of Transfiguration in Mark 9, and the Garden of Gethsemane in Matthew 26). In our passage we see them called upon to accompany Jesus into the house of Jairus. We cannot tell with what trepidation they entered. They could hear the sound of mourning and the crying of the family, and surely the Master had been told that it was too late to save the child.

As they entered, they saw the tenderness of the Saviour as He gently spoke to the young girl and invited her to rise. They heard Jesus tell the family to provide her with food and sustenance. Oh how often that tale must have been told in that town. How often the mourners would have told how their sorrow was turned into rejoicing, and how a wake became the greatest day of celebration that anyone could remember. For at the touch of Jesus, and a gentle word from His mouth, the dead were raised. Sickness banished. Death defeated. Sadness dismissed as easily as a servant was sent away. Master of disease, ruler of all sickness, and author of life.

What a thrill it must have been to travel with Jesus and to see such resounding evidence of the healing Jesus.

The healing miracles of Jesus made a terrific impact on the people of His day and continue to make that impact even today wherever the story is told.

21 And they came to Capernaum; and on the Sabbath he went into the Synagogue and gave teaching. 22 And they were full of wonder at his teaching, because he gave it as one having authority, and not like the scribes. 23 And there was in their Synagogue a man with an unclean spirit; and he gave a cry, 24 Saying, What have we to do with you, Jesus of Nazareth? have you come to put an end to us? I see well who you are, the Holy One of God. 25 And Jesus said to him sharply, Be quiet, and come out of him. 26 And the unclean spirit, shaking him violently, and crying with a loud voice, came out of him. 27 And they were all greatly surprised, so that they put questions to one another, saying, What is this? a new teaching! with authority he gives orders even to the unclean spirits, and they do what he says. 28 And news of him went out quickly everywhere into all parts of Galilee round about. 29 And when they came out of the Synagogue, they went into the house of Simon and Andrew, with James and John. 30 Now Simon's wife's mother was ill, with a burning heat; and they gave him word of her: 31 And he came and took her by the hand, lifting her up; and she became well, and took care of their needs. 32 And in the evening, at sundown,

they took to him all who were diseased, and those who had
evil spirits. 33 And all the town had come together at the
door. 34 And a number, who were ill with different diseases,
he made well, and sent out evil spirits; but he did not let the
evil spirits say anything, because they had knowledge of him.
Mark 1:21-34 BBE

The number of miracles performed by Jesus in these few verses cannot be calculated. It starts off simply enough with a man in the synagogue, and then the mother in law of Peter. However, by the end of our reading we see all the sick of that region being brought to Jesus; just how many was that? We cannot say. Were there ten, twenty, fifty, one hundred? No one can know. Not only are these miracles amazing in themselves, they are the miracles which so endeared Him to the people of His day. People loved Jesus because it was their neighbours and friends, their husbands and wives, their mothers and fathers who were ill and without hope, until the momentous day when they first met Jesus.

And so the healing Jesus is the abiding image for those who witnessed the ministry of the Master, and the draws all men to Him.

Called to a Healing Ministry:

No one ever healed like Jesus. Not before His coming and never since, has it been known that one could heal the ills, diseases, infirmities, and spiritual failings of man like Jesus could.

Not even the apostles healed like Jesus, though they were gifted with power from the same source.

But what we see in the gospel story is that healing went wherever Jesus went. And it seems to me that in a very real sense, wherever the gospel of Jesus goes, there is healing. For the mind is troubled in the life of the individual who lives without God, and the gospel brings peace to the troubled mind. The soul is sick and dead without God, and where the gospel goes there is healing of the soul. The more we think about this, the more we realize that when Jesus was healing people here on earth He had an even greater agenda than the healing of body and mind.

Indeed as we consider it we realize that the cleansing which comes through the blood of Christ heals both body and soul together.

- Man makes himself ill by sin.
- There is an abuse of the body caused by sin when alcohol and drugs ravage the body, bringing a soul to Christ takes that abuse out of the picture.
- There is an abuse of the body caused by sexual immorality and bringing a person to Christ removes that abuse from his or her life.
- There is an abuse of the body which is caused by strife and malice, and the torture of the body is removed when a man or woman gives themselves to Christ.
- There is a sickness of the mind which is caused by the unrelenting drive for material gain and profit, and the man or woman who gives themselves to Christ realizes that there is a gain in godliness which is far more important, and far more lasting. "There is great gain in godliness with contentment," says Paul.
- There is a sickness of the mind which is caused by what the Hebrew writer calls the bondage to the life-long fear of death. When a man is brought to Christ, it makes him realize that there is a life eternal which goes beyond the grave and even the grave is not something to be feared.

When he returned to Capernaum after some days, He was returning to His Galilean base and in effect it is reported that He was at home. Not the place of His birth and not the town where He was raised but His base of operations in Capernaum. So many gathered together that there was no room for them in the house where He was and they crowded around the door hoping to catch some wisdom from His lips.

Some people arrived carrying a friend who was paralysed. But they had no hope of getting him in through the doorway such was the great press of people. So they went up onto the flat roof of the house and pulling out the materials of which the roof was made they made an opening and lowered their friend down into the midst of the room. When Jesus saw what faith and hope lay behind their actions, he healed the man with a word. However the word was not what people expected to hear. "Your sins are forgiven you!" This indicated that Jesus was capable of dealing with both physical and spiritual problems. He could heal the sickness of the body and more important, He could heal the sickness of the soul. When some of the Jews wondered about this, Jesus challenged their thinking with these words, "which is easier to say, your sins are forgiven, or, stand up take up your bed and walk." The man picked up His bed healed of his physical and spiritual infirmities. (Read this in *Mark 2:1-12*)

This passage is one which is deeper than it first appears. We see immediately that Jesus seems to link the healing of the body and the removal of sin in some way. The possibilities are there to be considered and seen.

- Jesus is saying that to forgive sins was His prerogative. This I think would be agreed by all and is absolutely clear.
- Jesus is saying that His ability to heal the diseases of the body demonstrate His ability to also forgive sin because only God can do these things.
- Jesus presents Himself as the great healer of both body and soul.
- Men flocked to Him for the healing of the body, but He wanted them to realise that there is a healing of the soul which is even more important.

Wherever Jesus went there was healing of body and soul.
And wherever the gospel goes there is healing of body and soul.
Indeed, where the disciple of the Lord goes, there should go healing.
Think about it.

- When we bring someone into relationship with Christ it changes that life forever.
- It improves it beyond measure.
- It brings that life from turmoil to peace.
- It brings the troubled mind to the peace that passes all understanding.
- It delivers from abuse of body and mind to heavenly peace and health.

23 And may the God of peace himself make you holy in every way; and may your spirit and soul and body be free from all sin at the coming of our Lord Jesus Christ. 1 Thess 5:23 BBE

Through bringing Christ into the lives of men and women we bring them to peace with God and their fellow man. The Christian man has been brought to a lifestyle which is spiritually and physically healthy. The Christian woman has been brought to hope, purpose, and freedom from guilt. This preserves our mental health. In responding to the gospel, we are immersed into Christ and come to a cleansing which preserves our spiritual health and brings us into fellowship with God.

How can we then be like Jesus and let His story become our stories?

It is all a matter of bringing healing of the soul through the sharing of the gospel. Whenever we share the gospel and help people to come to faith in Jesus, we bring the healing of Jesus into their lives. Ours becomes the touch of healing because the gospel brings healing to men.

We are not peddling some dubious product, not double glazing or a mortgage, or an insurance policy—not that there is anything wrong with these things. But what we share is the gospel of Christ that brings transformation, healing, cleansing, eternal life, hope and spiritual sanity.

Some have a hard heart, closed to the needs of all others around us. The Lord knows how to give us a new heart.

Some are blind to the eternal truth of God, but in coming to know Jesus who is the truth, our sightless eyes are opened and we see the new kingdom of God, the amazing grace of God, and the glorious gospel of the Lord.

Let the healing story of Jesus become our story as we devote our lives to sharing the message of health and healing for today.

CHAPTER FOUR

Greater than Solomon

Every Bible hero gets known for their greatest quality. With Goliath it was his height. For Samson it was his strength. For David it was his courage. Job is remembered for his patience. If Solomon is known for one thing, it is his wisdom. The Queen of Sheba travelled hundreds of miles to speak with him, question him and ascertain whether his reputation was warranted. Solomon was a man with everything; wealth, talent, musical ability, poetic talent, extravagant building projects and horticultural developments (Read Ecclesiastes chapter 2). Yet all the glories of Solomon might pale to insignificance before the glory of someone else who was to come after him.

28 And why are you anxious about clothing? Consider the lilies of the field, how they grow: they neither toil nor spin, 29 yet I tell you, even Solomon in all his glory was not arrayed like one of these. 30 But if God so clothes the grass of the field, which today is alive and tomorrow is thrown into the oven, will he not much more clothe you, O you of little faith? Matt 6:28-31 ESV

42 On the Judgment Day the Queen of Sheba will stand up and accuse you, because she travelled all the way from her country to listen to King Solomon's wise teaching; and I assure you that there is something here greater than Solomon! Matt 12:42 TEV

In the above two passages we see the Old Testament king, Solomon, spoken of in the New Testament. In the first passage it was the splendour of his royal wardrobe, for Israel reached the greatest extent of its boundaries and became rich defeating their neighbours in battle. Almost unlimited resources were available to the king. Yet there is someone more glorious than Solomon. Not because of fashion or wardrobe but there is another who is clothed in robes of righteousness unparalleled in the history of the world.

Further Solomon is most remembered for his great wisdom. His rule was characterised by the gift of wisdom from God. His wisdom was so legendary that the Queen of Sheba came to investigate for herself and declared that the legend was understated rather than exaggerated. The half has not been told of his great wisdom. And yet, says the New Testament Scriptures, the wisdom of Jesus of Nazareth is far greater than this. A greater than Solomon is here, they declared.

Even some critics who do not believe that Jesus was the Son of God, would declare that the teachings of Jesus were the wisest way to live. Many who would not accept Jesus as Messiah, do accept Him as presenting the finest and best philosophy for life.

When Isaiah the prophet spoke—some seven hundred and fifty years before Christ—of the Messiah who was to come, there is a well known passage that declares of Him:

> *6 A child is born to us!*
> *A son is given to us!*
> *And he will be our ruler.*
> *He will be called, "Wonderful Counsellor,"*
> *"Mighty God," "Eternal Father,"*
> *"Prince of Peace."*
> *7 His royal power will continue to grow;*
> *His kingdom will always be at peace.*
> *He will rule as King David's successor,*
> *basing his power on right and justice,*
> *from now until the end of time.*
> *The Lord Almighty is determined to do all this. Isa 9:6-7 TEV*

We note that two of the four titles refer to the child who was to be born are divine titles (Mighty God, Eternal Father) because He is one with His Heavenly Father. The last refers to how He will rule in His Messianic kingdom. However the first is that He will be a counsellor for life beyond all others, a wonderful counsellor! His philosophy for life is above all others. His wisdom will guide our paths into fulfilled living, living the blessed life, the abundant life wherein is the peace that passes all understanding.

What makes His counsel so great? What makes His philosophy so different from all others? Let us select just a few examples of the kind of life He calls us to. Notice how He turns the worldly man's attitudes and assumptions upside down and declares this to be the secret of facing abundance and want, while remaining content.

The Philosophy of the Second Mile

The phrase "going the second mile" has entered into the English idiom and is used widely by many who have no idea of its origin. You may even have used it yourself before. Even in these days when people do not read the Bible quite so much as they used to, we still hear this phrase in common usage. Most who use it probably do not understand that it comes straight from the teaching of Jesus in the Sermon on the Mount. Here is the quote:

> *41 If a soldier demands that you carry his gear for a mile, carry it two miles. 42 Give to those who ask, and don't turn away from those who want to borrow. Matt 5:41-42 NLT.*

Palestine was an occupied country at the time of Jesus, part of the great Roman Empire. As such, Roman soldiers could compel a member of Israel to carry his burden for one mile, and by law they had to comply with the order.

The philosophy of Jesus is that we ought to do more than we are asked. If asked to carry the soldier's burden for one mile, carry it two. Think of this as a philosophy for life. What broad applications there are for this. What kind of employee would we make if we lived by this philosophy? Instead of just doing the minimum we can get away with as so many do, rather we look for the maximum we can accomplish for our employer. Would such a philosophy set you apart? What about our role as father or mother, husband or wife? Instead of following a policy of minima, just doing the least we can get away with, rather we serve one another to the highest and best of our ability. It is a policy of maxima rather than minima. I can say without fear of contradiction that if we follow a policy of going the second mile, we will be noticed for our generosity of spirit, and loving kindness. This is a revolutionary philosophy from the Wonderful Counsellor.

Philosophy of Turning the Other Cheek.

Again we notice that this is an expression which has become a common modern idiom. A bit of English language used very widely indeed which most will have forgotten comes from the mouth of the Master Teacher, the Wonderful Counsellor, Jesus.

What is this philosophy that Jesus is championing? Some would seek to rob it of its power by treating it with an absurd literalism. They would tell us that they have only two cheeks. They would offer the other cheek but after that the aggressor better watch out for that is when he will get it in the teeth! That would be to miss the point of the philosophy that Jesus is suggesting here.

Peter once questioned Jesus about how many times he should forgive another for an offence, whether physical or verbal? Look at how this brief conversation is recorded in the New Testament:

> *21 Then Peter came up and said to him, "Lord, how often will my brother sin against me, and I forgive him? As many as seven times?" 22 Jesus said to him, "I do not say to you seven times, but seventy times seven. Matt 18:21-22 ESV*

Some of the rabbis taught that one should forgive one's neighbour three times for sins against you. So when Peter made this suggestion to the Lord about forgiving seven times, he probably expected a commendation from the Lord for being so gracious. He had doubled the rabbinic tradition and added one on. Yet Jesus replied that seventy times seven would be more like the answer. He did not mean four hundred and ninety times but watch out on the four hundred and ninety first occasion you offend. The number is sufficiently large that no one could be expected to keep score to that level. Hence the Lord's teaching is to keep on forgiving indefinitely.

We know from our own experience that to withhold forgiveness, and hence bear a grudge in our hearts against another for their sins against us, harms us much more than it harms them. Hence the wisdom of this teaching about turning the other cheek is manifest. If we want to be healthy and happy within ourselves then we have to learn to be as forgiving as Jesus is forgiving. Jesus concludes this wisdom teaching with the telling of a parable in which we are instructed that we have been forgiven much by God, hence it would not make sense for us to refuse to forgive another.

I spoke recently with a grandmother whose granddaughter had been kidnapped and murdered by a man in England. She told me with tears in her eyes that she would never forgive that man. I replied that I hoped that one day she might be able to find it in her heart to forgive but I realised that it was no easy matter. (We ought not to judge people for situations we ourselves have never been through.) But the reason I hoped that for her was that her mind would never be able to be truly at rest until that day. To harbour ill will in the heart is far more injurious to us than it is to the object of our displeasure. We see the wisdom of the Wonderful Counsellor.

Philosophy of the Golden Rule.

Some might argue that the Golden Rule is one of the most significant statements ever uttered in terms of a life philosophy. In this Jesus stands head and shoulders above the rest and perhaps this is the concept for which He is best remembered. It is an excerpt from the Sermon on the Mount.

> 12 *"So whatever you wish that others would do to you, do also to them, for this is the Law and the Prophets. Matt 7:12 ESV*

Here is a simple, rule-of-thumb guide for behaviour: Ask yourself what you want people to do for you, then grab the initiative and do it for them. Can you imagine a society in which each member lived by this rule? Would not this be a blessed state in which to live? In fact such a society does exist. It is the new society of the kingdom of God, the realm in which Jesus reigns as king and is made up only of sincere disciples of the Lord Jesus Christ. In the kingdom of God there is love and peace. In the kingdom of God there is encouragement and kindness. In the kingdom of God there is no harm.

Isaiah the prophet spoke of this kingdom which was to come in Isa 35:8-10. This new way of the kingdom of God is likened to a highway through the desert. Only those who are cleansed by Christ can travel on that way, and it is so easy to follow that even the most dense among us can't go wrong, whilst travelling the way of Jesus. No one can harm us or overpower us when we stick to the narrow way, the way Christ calls us to come home. The only people we shall be with are those whom Christ has called and changed into His likeness. Ransomed from the futile ways of our past we shall come rejoicing together into heaven itself.

What a description of the Golden Rule society. It is a protected way (no lion shall strike). It is a holy way, and all who are upon it shall live their lives in a kingdom way (very often the Sermon on the Mount is referred to as the manifesto of the kingdom). All our fellow travellers are those who have committed their lives to Jesus and who want to live by the philosophies and concepts of Jesus of Nazareth for that is what it means to be a part of the great Kingdom of God.

The best that man can do is to come up with the Silver Rule. i.e. "Don't do harm to others because you wouldn't like it if they did harm to you." That's not a bad rule. But it is not in the same league as the Golden Rule. Listen to it again as it is rendered in some different translations.

> *12 "Do for others what you want them to do for you: this is the meaning of the Law of Moses and of the teachings of the prophets. Matt 7:12 GNT*

> *12 "Do for others what you want them to do for you. This is the teaching of the laws of Moses in a nutshell. Matt 7:12 TLB*

Philosophy of loving our enemies.

Each of these statements of philosophy for life are revolutionary and are capable of rendering society transformed. The more people there are living according to the wise teachings of Jesus, the more society is transformed. The more individuals there are who are transformed into living the Jesus way, the better place the world is. The big question is whether I will allow the philosophies of Jesus the Master Teacher to become my philosophy of life too.

Jesus states this new way of thinking, new way of living in Matt 5:43-48. Love your neighbour and hate your enemy? Anyone can do that. I say to you, love your enemies. This is amazing, Jesus. This is a revolutionary new way of living.

Love your enemies! Now that is revolutionary. It is almost unimaginable, unthinkable. How can someone truly love their enemies? Perhaps we need to talk about the meaning of the word love for a moment or two to try to get our bearings on this revolutionary new thought. In English, we have one word, "love". And we use it to describe how we feel about our children, our spouse, or ice cream and jelly. Clearly it is a very broad word.

The Greeks (the original language in which the New Testament was written) have four words for love. First they have the term *"eros"* from which we get the word "erotic" in English. This is the word for sexual love. Not surprisingly that is not the word used by Jesus in this passage. Jesus is not commanding that we should feel about our enemies like we want to have sex with them.

Second they have the word *"storge"* which is the word for family love. This is how you might feel about your parents, or children. Jesus did not use that word in this passage either. We might conclude that it would not be possible for us to feel about our enemies in the same way that we feel about our children.

Third is the word *"philia"* from which we get the English philanthropy (love for man). Vine translates this as "tender affection". It is the word used in the New Testament for the tender affection that Jesus had for His apostle, John. John was probably the youngest of the disciples of Jesus, and in some ways the most devoted. His devotion to Jesus took him to the foot of the cross, and when Jesus looked down from the cross only John, among His apostles, was there. The others had fled. This word is used in the name of the city Philadelphia. *Adelphos* is the Greek word for brother and hence the name of that place is supposed to indicate the city of brotherly love. That is not the word used here by Jesus either.

Finally we come to the fourth word *"Agape"*. It is not so much a feeling as an act of will. It is difficult to command feelings anyway, though that which is an action may be commanded. This is the word most often used to describe God's love for us. Barclay, the world renowned Greek scholar from Glasgow University, described this word as meaning "unconquerable benevolence". In other words, no matter what you might do to me, I am going to seek your highest good. It is the word used in the New Testament to describe the attitude of the Heavenly Father towards His Son Jesus. It is also used to describe what God's will is for His children concerning their attitude towards one another. This is the word that Jesus uses to describe how we are to treat our enemies. God calls us to this as a philosophy for life because it is how He is. It is His philosophy. It is that which caused Jesus to pray for those who were engaged in crucifying Him, "Forgive them for they know not what they do."

Where is this new kingdom of God? That is the kind of society I want to belong to. The answer may surprise you. The answer is the church for right now, and heaven in eternity. The church? Perhaps we don't think about the church in that way. Yet that is why Jesus thought the church so important, so relevant to life today. It would be the place where Christianity was put in the shop window, a show case of living the Jesus way.

There may be some who are untransformed, un-regenerated, but that does not take away from the fact that the church is the showcase-society and there *are* many who are living life in the new way, walking that high and holy way that Isaiah spoke of, and you will find them in the church. It is the place where "the ransomed of the Lord" are. Not even fools can go too far astray there, when they walk in company with those whose lives have been transformed by the wise teaching of the Master and the indwelling of the Spirit of God. This is internal revolution.

Each of these sayings we have been looking at came from Jesus' famous teachings in the Sermon on the Mount. When Jesus declared these life principles, the people realised they had never heard anything like it before. Looking at the end of the Sermon on the Mount we read these words.

> *24 "Therefore whoever hears these sayings of Mine, and does them, I will liken him to a wise man who built his house on the rock: 25 and the rain descended, the floods came, and the winds blew and beat on that house; and it did not fall, for it was founded on the rock.*
>
> *26 "But everyone who hears these sayings of Mine, and does not do them, will be like a foolish man who built his house on the sand: 27 and the rain descended, the floods came, and the winds blew and beat on that house; and it fell. And great was its fall."*
>
> *28 And so it was, when Jesus had ended these sayings, that the people were astonished at His teaching, 29 for He taught them as one having authority, and not as the scribes. Matt 7:24-29 NKJV*

We can understand the reaction of the people. Where did this man get all this? This is brand new. A new way of living. The secret of the blessed life... the secret of living the way God intends us to live.

A Parable:

Here is a silly story with a deeper meaning than is first perceived. There was this world in which the people all lived in darkness. People regularly fell over things and hurt themselves. They walked into holes and hollows along the pathway and broke bones and cut themselves with monotonous regularity. However, that was all they knew.

One day a wonderful teacher appeared on the scene and told them of a different way to live. He would supply them with a miner's helmet which would become a light to their path and a lamp for their feet. No more falling in the ditch. No more cuts and bruises. All they had to do was wear the helmet. The teacher said, "follow me and you will have the light of life." Life was certainly a lot less dangerous with the lights on. There were much fewer injuries and people began to gather a sense of knowing where they were and where they were going.

Sadly, there were some of the disciples of the good teacher who came to the conclusion that they looked "different" from everyone else. Some felt the helmet was not quite the right look for them. It didn't really suit them. It was more fashionable to have cuts and bruises. So they took the helmets off and went back to what they were like before.

Thankfully, more and more people could see that having the light of life, having a lamp for our feet was of infinitely more value than cuts and bruises. For the first time in their lives, they knew where they were and where they were going.

If we think of Solomon as the wisest man who ever lived, and hence he might become for us a wonderful counsellor for life, then truly a greater than Solomon is here.

CHAPTER FIVE

Jesus the Great Sacrifice

Vilest sin, vexed God, virtuous Christ. Vilest sin was man's downfall. Virtuous Christ is God's solution. The story of the Bible can be expressed as a great unfolding drama (one author referring to it as the "unfolding drama of redemption"), the story of how a loving God decided to reach out to man sinking in the swamp of his own sinfulness. God reached out a loving hand to pull us free from the quicksand of bad habits and worse decisions and provided for us a way of escape.

The prophet Isaiah spoke of this solution some seven hundred plus years before the events of Calvary. He was wounded because of our shortcomings. We have been wandering along through life with no spiritual direction and no clue about how to live life right. He was bruised because of our wrongdoings (Isa 53:5-7).

We are looking in this chapter at statements from the mouth of Isaiah which are the very heart of the gospel, for the cross is the very heart of the gospel. It speaks of:

- The depth of human need for rescue from the prison-house of wrong-doing.
- The corruptness of the human spirit
- The plan of God laid down before time began
- The depths of the punishment received by the Messiah
- The suffering of Christ experienced in order to deal with the problem of our guilt.

All of these things are emphasized in this short passage of Scripture. Guilt, culpability, pardon, forgiveness and cleansing.

All we like sheep have gone astray:

Isaiah emphasizes the universal nature of the problem. It is not just something which we can see lots of examples of; it is not just something which is fairly widespread. It is universal across the human race. All we like sheep have gone astray.

But in the brutal death of Jesus of Nazareth, God somehow or other set things right. He took the pain and the punishment, the guilt and shame. Wonder of wonders, I got forgiveness, a clean slate, welcome into the embrace of God. How is all of that possible? That is the wonder of the grace of God, and the love of Jesus (Rom 3:21-24).

No man can say that the death of Christ is nothing to do with me. The passage presents the universal need for forgiveness. I need to be forgiven. You need to be forgiven. Indeed that is what the sacrifice of Jesus is all about. There is a right way and all have strayed from it. I need a Saviour. You need a Saviour.

The human race is pictured as a flock of lost sheep. They are carried this way and that by the whims of the moment or the elementary pressures of the environment. There is no grand plan or eternal course which they follow but are carried by the momentary desires of one blade of grass or another; or because some noise frightens them and drives them in a particular direction.

Isaiah makes the point that this waywardness, and fickleness is serious because it affects the moral choices we make. We have erred, gone astray, sinned.

The Lord has laid on Him the shortcomings of us all:

Isaiah stresses the absolute necessity of the sacrifice of Christ. In this short phrase we have encapsulated the grace of God.

- Though I am undeserving,
- though I am spiritually weak not spiritually strong,

- though I am a sinner not a righteous person,
- though I was formerly an enemy of the cross of Christ,

yet still the Lord has laid on Him, all of my iniquities.

God did not select those who were specially religious or extraordinarily holy to be a recipient of His grace. Christ died for *us*.

> *6 When we were utterly helpless, with no way of escape, Christ came at just the right time and died for us sinners who had no use for him. 7 Even if we were good, we really wouldn't expect anyone to die for us, though, of course, that might be barely possible. 8 But God showed his great love for us by sending Christ to die for us while we were still sinners. 9 And since by his blood he did all this for us as sinners, how much more will he do for us now that he has declared us not guilty? Now he will save us from all of God's wrath to come. 10 And since, when we were his enemies, we were brought back to God by the death of his Son, what blessings he must have for us now that we are his friends and he is living within us! 11 Now we rejoice in our wonderful new relationship with God-all because of what our Lord Jesus Christ has done in dying for our sins-making us friends of God. Rom 5:6-11 TLB*

You can tell that the words of Isaiah were preying on the mind of the Apostle Peter when he penned these words:

> *21 It was to this that God called you, for Christ himself suffered for you and left you an example, so that you would follow in his steps. 22 He committed no sin, and no one ever heard a lie come from his lips. 23 When he was insulted, he did not answer back with an insult; when he suffered, he did not threaten, but placed his hopes in God, the righteous Judge. 24 Christ himself carried our sins in his body to the cross, so that we might die to sin and live for righteousness. It is by his wounds that you have been healed. 25 You were like*

> *sheep that had lost their way, but now you have been brought*
> *back to follow the Shepherd and Keeper of your souls. 1 Peter*
> *2:21-25 TEV*

This is the central concept of the gospel. Jesus died taking the guilt of our sins that we might receive by faith the righteousness which comes from Him as a gift. He takes our sin and we take His righteousness.

> *22 We are made right with God by placing our faith in Jesus*
> *Christ. And this is true for everyone who believes, no matter*
> *who we are. 23 For everyone has sinned; we all fall short*
> *of God's glorious standard. 24 Yet God, with undeserved*
> *kindness, declares that we are righteous. He did this through*
> *Christ Jesus when he freed us from the penalty for our sins.*
> *25 For God presented Jesus as the sacrifice for sin. People are*
> *made right with God when they believe that Jesus sacrificed*
> *his life, shedding his blood. This sacrifice shows that God*
> *was being fair when he held back and did not punish those*
> *who sinned in times past, 26 for he was looking ahead and*
> *including them in what he would do in this present time.*
> *God did this to demonstrate his righteousness, for he himself*
> *is fair and just, and he declares sinners to be right in his sight*
> *when they believe in Jesus. Rom 3:22-26 NLT*

Christ is the way to holiness for unholy man.

Indeed in Christ we have the fulfilment and the completion of all the sacrificial ministry of all the Old Testament priests who ever lived. He became the perfect High Priest for us. As the Hebrew writer put it, He became our sacrifice on that great and perfect Day of Atonement.

Wounded for our Disobedience:

The Bible leaves us in no doubt as to where the guilt lies. It does not lie with Jesus, but with us. The word which is translated as transgressions in some versions of the Bible is a word which means stepping over the line. It carries with it the suggestion of a deliberate action. We know where the line is and we deliberately step over it. Of course if we are brutally honest about it, stepping over the line is something that has been part of our repertoire. It is exactly what we have done. There have been many times when we knew what right and wrong were and we made a choice to do that which is wrong. This represents a state of rebellion against God. But God loved us so much He did not want to leave us in that rebellious state. After all, one day we shall face Him and we shall either face Him as rebels or friends. Christ came and took the guilt and the punishment for our transgressions, so that we could come on that day into the presence of God as friends.

What the prophet wants us to see is that there is a direct connection between the suffering of Christ on the cross and our disobedience. The reason why Jesus had to go through such dreadful wounding was because our sin was a problem which was separating us from God and from an eternity in heaven. The only way to deal with that was if Jesus was wounded in our stead. When the spear was thrust into His side, it should have been mine. When the scourge ripped the flesh off His back, it was yours that deserved such punishment. For He had no guilt, the guilt was mine, mine and yours. He had perfect holiness, we had shortcomings. Hence the punishment He took, He took for us. The wound of the spear in His side was the means by which the blood flowed, and the flowing of the blood was necessary for the cleansing away of sin. When we are united with Christ in His death, then we are brought into contact with His blood, and then we are cleansed of sin. We must be united with Christ in His death, in His burial and in His resurrection in order to receive that cleansing.

> *3 For surely you know that when we were baptized into union with Christ Jesus, we were baptized into union with his death. 4 By our baptism, then, we were buried with him and shared his death, in order that, just as Christ was raised from death by the glorious power of the Father, so also we might live a new life.*

> *5 For since we have become one with him in dying as he did, in the same way we shall be one with him by being raised to life as he was. 6 And we know that our old being has been put to death with Christ on his cross, in order that the power of*

the sinful self might be destroyed, so that we should no longer be the slaves of sin. 7 For when we die, we are set free from the power of sin. 8 Since we have died with Christ, we believe that we will also live with him. 9 For we know that Christ has been raised from death and will never die again — death will no longer rule over him. 10 And so, because he died, sin has no power over him; and now he lives his life in fellowship with God. 11 In the same way you are to think of yourselves as dead, so far as sin is concerned, but living in fellowship with God through Christ Jesus. Rom 6:3-11 GNT

Bruised for our Offences:

In some Bibles the word "iniquity" is used. Its root meaning is that it refers literally to a "false step" or blunder. This is the situation when we don't necessarily set out to do that which is wrong but that is the result anyway. We perhaps do not plan to do evil, but we blunder our way into it anyway. It seems like we have a kind of special talent for opening our mouth and putting our foot in it. We did not mean harm but we caused it nonetheless.

When we consider the treatment of Jesus during those last few hours of His physical life, the injuries sustained were horrific and excruciating. Isaiah with a sense of restraint says, He was bruised for our iniquities. Perhaps Isaiah is influenced by the statement which is the first prophecy of the Christ in Scripture. It comes rather surprisingly in Gen 3. Jesus as the seed of woman is mentioned and His suffering alluded to (Gen 3:15).

The Messiah would receive a bruise to the heel. i.e. He would be injured but not overcome nor defeated. The devil would have an injury rather to the head, a death blow from which he would never recover. And so Satan is defeated by the action of the Christ on the cross, his power restricted by the sacrifice Messiah gave.

Pilate took Jesus and had him whipped, almost to within an inch of His life. The soldiers took Jesus away and braided together a mock crown of large thorns. They pressed it down into His skull. Then in mocking mode they threw an old cloak around His shoulders and saluted Him as king. When they were finished with all of that they slapped Him in the face (*John 19:2-3*). They took Jesus away to the place they called the skull (because of the profile of the hill). It was just outside the city walls and there they crucified Him. There were two others, criminals, perhaps deserving of death. In a moment of rash honesty, Pilate had a sign made up to put on the cross which read, "Jesus of Nazareth, the King of the Jews." (John 19:16-19)

Even unintended evil can be cleansed by the sacrifice of our Suffering Servant.

With His stripes we are healed:

What does this statement mean? The stripes are the marks on His tortured body. He received a scourging at the hands of Roman soldiers. The healing is ours and the punishment His. Isaiah now speaks of the Christ, "With His stripes we are healed." The injuries caused by the scourging and by the crucifixion were horrific. No one in ancient times needed to be reminded of that fact. Today it takes a viewing of *The Passion* movie to remind us that the effects on a human body were catastrophic. It was not unknown for a man to die under the effects of scourging. The strands of the scourge often would have small pieces of metal or stone attached in order to rip at the flesh and strip it off the back of the prisoner. The marks on the body are here described as stripes.

Jesus was tortured on the tree, that we might be free from sin, that we might find healing from the deadly disease of the soul, sin.

Yet He opened not His mouth (v7):

This phrase is used twice in one verse(Isa 53:7), emphasizing the deliberate nature of the Lord's death. He did not try to avoid it. This was what He came to do. He laid down His life in a very deliberate way (John 10:14-18). "I lay down my life and I will pick it up."

And so when it came to the trials of Jesus, He did not attempt to avoid His fate. He came in order to give His life as a ransom for many. He would not defend Himself (not in terms of offering a verbal rebuttal to the charges laid, nor in terms of calling upon the vast resources at His disposal).

Notice Jesus in the presence of His accusers:

1. Matt 26:62-64. Before Caiaphas.

> *62 The High Priest stood up and said to Jesus, "Have you no answer to give to this accusation against you?" 63 But Jesus kept quiet. Again the High Priest spoke to him, "In the name of the living God I now put you under oath: tell us if you are the Messiah, the Son of God." 64 Jesus answered him, "So you say. But I tell all of you: from this time on you will see the Son of Man sitting at the right side of the Almighty and coming on the clouds of heaven!" Matt 26:62-64 GNT*

This is the opposite of a defence. Jesus refuses to answer the High Priest, and turns the words of the High Priest upon himself.

2. Matt 27:11-14. Before Pilate.

> *11 Jesus stood before the Roman governor, who questioned him. "Are you the king of the Jews?" he asked. "So you say," answered Jesus. 12 But he said nothing in response to the accusations of the chief priests and elders.*
> *13 So Pilate said to him, "Don't you hear all these things they accuse you of?"*
> *14 But Jesus refused to answer a single word, with the result that the Governor was greatly surprised. TEV*

Before the Roman governor Jesus would not open his mouth to offer any defence once again. The governor had never come across such a thing. Usually there would be some kind of pleading on such charges. The death penalty was on the cards and yet the defendant offered no explanation, no extenuating circumstances, no defence of any kind.

3. Matt 27:28-30. Before soldiers.

> *27 The governor's soldiers took Jesus into the governor's palace,*
> *and they all gathered around him. 28 They took off his clothes*
> *and put a red robe on him. 29 Using thorny branches, they*
> *made a crown, put it on his head, and put a stick in his right*
> *hand. Then the soldiers bowed before Jesus and made fun of*
> *him, saying, "Hail, King of the Jews!" 30 They spat on Jesus.*
> *Then they took his stick and began to beat him on the head.*
> *31 After they finished, the soldiers took off the robe and put*
> *his own clothes on him again. Then they led him away to be*
> *crucified. NCV*

Before the whole company of soldiers, Jesus is mocked. Remember His behaviour in other circumstances, clearing the temple, when they came as an armed troupe to the garden to arrest Him, etc. Jesus was capable of making an imposing presence and defence of His situation. He could at any time have called upon ten thousand angels to defeat any force the Jewish or Roman authorities could put forward. And yet in these occasions He like a sheep before its shearers is dumb, so He opened not His mouth. He restrained Himself. He restrained His omnipotence and accepted gracefully this mockery and ill treatment.

4. Luke 23:8-9. Before Herod.

> *Luke 23:8-10*
> *8 When Herod saw Jesus, he was very glad, for he had long*
> *desired to see him, because he had heard about him, and he*
> *was hoping to see some sign done by him. 9 So he questioned*
> *him at some length, but he made no answer. ESV*

Herod was a very dangerous man. However Jesus is placed in a position where perhaps by the performing of a few miracles, He might have been able to sway Herod to release Him. Yet like a lamb led to the slaughter, He opened not His mouth. This is the reason He came. He came to bring about your redemption. He came in order that He might be *wounded for our transgressions, bruised for our iniquities, that by His stripes we might be healed.*

Jesus died that we might live.

Jesus suffered that we might soar.

Jesus took on our sin, that we might take on His righteousness.

The hymn writer perhaps said it better than any of us could...

> Man of sorrows, what a name
> For the Son of God who came
> Ruined sinners to reclaim.
> Hallelujah what a Saviour.
>
> Bearing shame and scoffing rude
> In my place condemned He stood.
> Sealed my pardon with His blood,
> Hallelujah what a Saviour.
>
> Guilty, vile and helpless, we
> Spotless Lamb of God was He;
> Full atonement, can it be,
> Hallelujah what a Saviour.
>
> Lifted up was He to die.
> It is finished was His cry.
> Now in heaven exalted high
> Hallelujah, what a Saviour!
>
> When He comes our glorious King,
> All His ransomed home to bring
> Then anew this song we'll sing
> Hallelujah what a Saviour.

P. P. Bliss.

CHAPTER SIX

The Empty Tomb.

Empty. The tomb was empty. He had been laid there only three days before and a guard had been placed on the tomb, because the man had to be silenced, didn't he? It could not go on. Really it could not go on, because everyone would end up believing in Him and we would have lost our place.

This was the thinking of the Jewish authorities. Most movements, begun by mere mortal man soon run out of steam as soon as the man is removed from this world's scene. This is certainly not true of Jesus and Christianity. Most movements can point to the grave of the instigator of the movement. But in the case of Jesus, the tomb was empty, a mere three days after His undignified and scandalous death on a Roman cross. Perhaps this is the most powerful statement of all about this Jesus of Nazareth. This is the ultimate, the crux of the matter.

Is the bodily resurrection of Christ a true event of history or is it the false base for a false religion? Both friends and enemies of the Christian faith have recognized the resurrection of Christ to be the foundation stone of the faith.

Paul in writing to the Corinthians said this:

> ... *if Christ is not risen, then our preaching is empty and your faith is also empty. 1 Cor 15:14-15 NKJV*

Either the resurrection is the greatest event in human history in which man finds his ultimate salvation, or it is the greatest and cruellest of illusions. It is either the greatest act in all history or that which has duped many to go to a meaningless death. If He did rise, it was the most sensational event in the history, and we have conclusive answers to the profound questions of our existence. Where have we come from? Why are we here? Where are we going?

If Christ arose, we know with certainty that God exists, what He is like, and how we may know Him personally. The Risen Christ means we have to make a revision to our worldview and take into account all that Jesus taught us. The universe takes on meaning and purpose, and it is possible to experience the living God in contemporary Dundee, Glasgow, Leeds or Delhi.

However, if He did not rise from the dead then Christianity is an interesting anachronism, a strange museum piece, nothing more. It has no objective validity or reality. The martyrs who went singing to the lions, and even in the last century, those missionaries who gave their lives willingly were nothing more than poor deluded fools.

Hence the doctrine of the resurrection of the Christ is either the greatest good for mankind or one of the greatest evils. It cannot be anything in between.

We should note that the concept of the resurrection did not develop accidentally. Neither was it an idle tale invented by the disciples. This is because Jesus repeatedly made reference to his death and resurrection during the three and a half years of his public ministry.

> *19 Jesus answered them, "Destroy this temple, and in three days I will raise it up." 20 The Jews then said, "It took forty-six years to build this temple, and will You raise it up in three days?" 21 But He was speaking of the temple of His body. 22 So when He was raised from the dead, His disciples remembered that He said this; and they believed the Scripture and the word which Jesus had spoken. John 2:19-22 NASU*

> *"An evil and adulterous generation craves for a sign; and yet no sign shall be given to it but the sign of Jonah the prophet; 40 for just as Jonah was three days and three nights in the belly of the sea monster, so shall the Son of Man be three days*

and three nights in the heart of the earth. Matt 12:39-41
NASB

30 Jesus and his disciples left that place and went on through
Galilee. Jesus did not want anyone to know where he was, 31
because he was teaching his disciples: "The Son of Man will
be handed over to those who will kill him. Three days later,
however, he will rise to life." Mark 9:30-31 RSV

30 Jesus and his disciples left that place and went on through
Galilee. Jesus did not want anyone to know where he was, 31
because he was teaching his disciples: "The Son of Man will
be handed over to those who will kill him. Three days later,
however, he will rise to life." Mark 9:30-31 GNT

We note that Jesus staked His whole credibility on the idea that He would rise again. If He was not raised, then we should not listen to Him. If, though, He was indeed raised—if after three days that tomb was indeed empty—then it validates everything He ever said and taught us. For that reason, we should listen to Him with full attention, for He has the words of life and is indeed our hope and our salvation.

Take time to read John chapters 19, 20 and 21. If you are in a home Bible study now, share the reading with others in the room. Read it prayerfully and carefully, considering the experience of Jesus as He gave His life as a ransom for all. This is a poignant and powerful account. This is what Jesus said would be that which would draw all men to Him.

In the 1930s, a remarkable attack on the resurrection was launched by a young British lawyer. He was convinced that the resurrection was a mere tissue of fable and fantasy. Sensing that it was the foundation stone of the Christian faith, he decided to do the world a favour by once and for all exposing this fraud and superstition. As a lawyer, he felt he had the critical faculties to sift the evidence and to admit nothing as evidence which did not meet the stiff criteria for admission into a law court.

However, while he was doing his research a remarkable thing happened. The case was not nearly as easy as he had supposed. As a result, the first chapter of his book is entitled, "The Book That Refused to Be Written."

In it he describes how as he examined the evidence, he became persuaded against his will, of the fact of the bodily resurrection. The book is called "Who Moved the Stone?" and the author is Frank Morrison. It has become a classic defence of the resurrection of Jesus.

There are in fact two vital parts to the evidence concerning the resurrection of Christ.

1. The Empty Tomb
2. The Resurrection Appearances.

Both of these pieces of evidence require to be examined before we close our mind to the case. The court is now assembled, the witnesses are gathered, we are the jury, let us hear the case and decide the verdict. In so doing, we make the most important judgment of our lives.

The Empty Tomb.

Other religions have shrines where their leaders were buried, but Christianity stands unique amongst the religions of the world for what it has is an empty tomb. This fact has to be reckoned with, and since the events of that fateful weekend in Jerusalem, friends and foes of Christianity have been making their arguments about the empty tomb. How can we account for the empty tomb?

There have been only a few reasoned suggestions made to account for the empty tomb and we shall examine these briefly:

a. Disciples stole the body.

This was the earliest explanation that was circulated. It was the reaction of the chief priests and the elders when the guards gave them the infuriating and mysterious news that the body was gone.

> *11 Now while they were on their way, behold, some of the*
> *guard came into the city and reported to the chief priests all*
> *that had happened. 12 And when they had assembled with*
> *the elders and counselled together, they gave a large sum of*
> *money to the soldiers, 13 and said, "You are to say, 'His*

disciples came by night and stole Him away while we were asleep.' 14 "And if this should come to the governor's ears, we will win him over and keep you out of trouble." 15 And they took the money and did as they had been instructed; and this story was widely spread among the Jews, and is to this day.
Matthew 28:11-15 NASB

They gave the soldiers money and told them to explain that the disciples had come at night and stolen the body whilst they were asleep. That story is such an obvious fabrication that Matthew does not even bother to refute it. What judge would listen to you if you said that whilst you were asleep your neighbour came into your house and stole your television set? How would you know what had happened if you were asleep at the time? Testimony like this would be laughed out of court.

There were two further things wrong with this theory. First of all, it was foreign to the ethical standards and behaviour of the disciples. It would mean that they were perpetrators of a deliberate lie, which was responsible for the ultimate deaths of thousands of people. That is not the character of the disciples of Jesus. Second, it should be remembered that these disciples gave their own lives for their testimony concerning the empty tomb. It is one thing to tell a lie to deceive others, but to go to death yourself for something you know to be a lie is beyond belief. If the disciples had actually stolen the body, surely they would have told the truth on the point of death and rescued themselves.

b. Authorities stole the body.

The second hypothesis was that the authorities, either Jewish or Roman stole the body. But why? Having put guards at the tomb, what would have been their reason for removing the body? And what is even more damning to this theory is, why—after the disciples began to declare the resurrection message—did they remain silent? Why did they not immediately speak up and declare it all to be a trick, and produce the body, dragging it through the streets of Jerusalem so that everyone could see and should give no credence to the declaration of resurrection appearances?

That would have been a very simple solution to all their problems. The authorities could have strangled Christianity in its cradle, and it would never have grown to be believed throughout the world as it is today. They could not do it though, because they did not have the body to produce. They were mystified as to what they could do. They arrested the apostles (Acts 4) and they threatened them, instructing them to desist from telling the resurrection message. But no matter how hard they tried, they could not silence it. They could not silence the eloquent testimony of an empty tomb. Their guards and seals had been set in an attempt to stop the tomb being empty. But no guards or seals could withstand the Christ's resurrection.

c. The Wrong Tomb.

A third theory propounded was that the women went to the wrong tomb. Those women were distraught and overcome with grief, and in the early morning gloom, they simply went to the wrong tomb. In their distress, they imagined that Jesus had risen because they found an empty tomb.

However, this theory is very easily destroyed. If the women went to the wrong tomb, why did not the disciples go to the right tomb? Even more important, why did not the Jews and Romans simply point out the mistake as soon as the preaching of resurrection occurred. Certainly Joseph of Arimathea, the owner of the tomb could have settled the matter once and for all. Further it should be remembered that this was not some large uniform public cemetery with a thousand graves all the same. There was no other tomb there that would have allowed them to make a mistake.

d. The Swoon Theory.

The swoon theory was a fourth hypothesis which has been put forward. In this view, Christ did not actually die. He was mistakenly reported as dead, but He had in fact fainted, and (they say) in the coolness of the tomb He revived and came out of the tomb, appearing to the disciples who mistakenly reported Him as risen from the dead. This is a theory of modern construction. It first appeared at the end of the eighteenth century.

Not one suggestion has come down from antiquity of this nature. But for the sake of argument, let us assume that they are right. Jesus did not actually die, but swooned.

He survived three days in the tomb without....

- medical attention despite His horrific wounds
- water
- food or any other sustenance to revive Him

It should be remembered that He survived swathed in burial clothes which were covered in burial spices. Could He have survived in such circumstances?

- Where did He get the strength to get out of the burial clothes?
- Where did He get the strength to push the huge stone away from the front of the tomb?
- How did He get past the guards that had been placed there?
- And once He had done that how did He then walk miles on feet that had been pierced with spikes to get away from the district?

Even some of Christianity's fiercest critics have been scathing about the viability of this theory. David Strauss, the German critic, who does not believe in the resurrection, rejected the idea as incredible. He said, *"It is impossible that one who had just come forth from the grave, half dead, who crept about weak and ill, who stood in the need of medical treatment, of bandaging, strengthening, and tender care, and who at last succumbed to suffering, could ever have given the disciples the impression that He was a conqueror over death and the grave; that He was the Prince of Life".* Finally of course, if this theory is correct, Christ Himself was involved in flagrant lies. His disciples believed He had been dead and come back to life, Jesus did nothing to dispel this thought, indeed He commended those who accepted this and encouraged them to go throughout the world preaching it.

When each of the theories is examined in turn, we find nothing to commend them. Rather we see that reliable witnesses testified that the dead Christ rose, that the tomb was empty on that Sunday morning. They suffered death rather than change their testimony by one sentence, one word, or one comma. We have the kind of evidence that would be acceptable in any court of law, in any country, in any age. The empty tomb proclaims the risen Christ, then and now, and its evidence is incontrovertible.

Other hallmarks of authenticity.

Another important consideration is that the claim that Jesus had risen from the dead was first published in the very city where it was reported to have happened and no one was able to disprove it or contradict it. Suppose the resurrection was alleged to have happened in Glasgow, Scotland and was first declared and preached in Delhi, India! We might say that we would only have the words of those people in Delhi who proclaimed it. How could they know? How do we know that these things are so because Glasgow is a long way away. We can't go to the tomb; we can't talk to the witnesses.

We see that He rose in Jerusalem and the preaching began there amongst the witnesses and all could go to the garden tomb and assure themselves it was indeed empty. Clearly the people who were closest to the event in history and who would most assuredly have wanted to put a stop to such a report were powerless in the face of the facts at hand. The Apostles preached a resurrected Christ in a place and at a time when it was fully possible to check every piece of evidence, to interrogate every witness and to expose any trace of fraud.

The only reasonable conclusion is that they were telling the truth and had nothing to fear from an investigation of their claim. Many of the Apostles spent their whole lives preaching the resurrected Christ under the most difficult and trying of circumstances. They were cursed, hated, driven out of cities, imprisoned and tortured because of their message. Many died as martyrs. Would this group of men have been so motivated by a story which they knew to be a lie? You know that is absurd.

The Resurrection Appearances.

During the forty day period between His resurrection and ascension, there were ten recorded appearances that the Lord made to various individuals under different circumstances:

i. Appeared to three women who came to the tomb. (Matthew 28:10)
ii. Appeared to Mary Magdalene. (John 20:11-18)
iii. Appeared to Simon Peter. (Luke 24:34)
iv. Appeared to two disciples on road to Emmaus. (Luke 24:13-35)
v. Appeared to ten disciples in locked room with Thomas absent. (John 20:19-25)
vi. Appeared to the eleven with Thomas present. (John 20:26-29)
vii. Appeared to disciples as they were fishing. (John 21:1-23)
viii. Appeared to five hundred brethren at one time. (1 Corinthians 15:6)
ix. Appeared to James. (1 Corinthians 15:7)
x. Appeared to all the disciples at the time of His ascension on the Mount of Olives. (Luke 24:50-52, Acts 1:3-10)

We see that there is a great diversity in the circumstances, timing and location of the appearances of Jesus. Some were in the garden near His tomb; some were in the upper room. One was on the road from Jerusalem to Emmaus, and some were far away in Galilee.

The major theory advanced to explain away the accounts of Christ is that they were hallucinations. At first this sounds like a plausible explanation of an otherwise supernatural event. Let us think about this explanation for a moment.

Hallucinations occur generally in people who tend to be vividly imaginative and of a nervous disposition. But the appearances of Christ were to all sorts of people. True, some could be accused of being emotional or excitable, but there were also hard-headed men like fishermen, a tax collector, and others of various dispositions.

Hallucinations are extremely subjective and individual. For this reason no two people have the same experience. But in the case of the resurrection, Christ appeared not just to individuals, but to groups, including one of more than 500 people.

Hallucinations usually occur only at particular times and places and are associated with regular events remembered. But these appearances occurred both indoors and outdoors, in the morning, afternoon and evening.

If only Peter and James and John had claimed to have seen Christ and no other witnesses, we might think that these three who had been so close to Jesus were so emotionally distraught over the events of their friend's death that they hallucinated. But there were hundreds of people involved as witnesses of the living Christ. They saw Him at different times and under different circumstances, but they were all positive in their identification.

Generally psychic experiences like this occur over a long period of time and with some regularity. But these experiences happened during a period of forty days and then stopped abruptly. No one ever said they happened again. Who cured these people of their hallucinations?

Finally, we must note that in order to have an experience like this, one must so intensely want to believe that he projects something that really isn't there and attaches reality to his imagination. Suppose for instance a mother who has lost her son in the war remembers how he used to come home from work every evening at six o'clock. She sits in her rocking chair every afternoon musing and remembering. Finally she thinks she sees him come through the door at that time and has a conversation with him. At this point she has lost touch with reality.

But this was not the case with the disciples of Jesus. The women came with ointments to complete the burial. And when He appeared to them they did not believe it thinking that He was the gardener. They were brought to belief against their expectation. When the other disciples heard, the Scripture says,

> *11 but the apostles didn't believe a word of it, thought they were making it all up.*
> *12 But Peter jumped to his feet and ran to the tomb. He stooped to look in and saw a few grave clothes, that's all. He walked away puzzled, shaking his head. Luke 24:11-12 (THE MESSAGE.)*

Of course, the classic case is that of Thomas, who was not present on the first occasion when Jesus appeared to the disciples in a locked room. They told him about it and he scoffed and said that unless he could feel the nail prints he would not believe. The story of what happened is told in John 20. Jesus appeared to him and invited him to touch and believe. Thomas fell down in worship and declared, *"My Lord and my God."*

To hold the hallucination theory in explaining the appearances of Christ, one must completely ignore the evidence.

Conclusion:

The most remarkable event of all history is declared by the empty tomb and the eyewitness testimony concerning a risen Christ. This is the bedrock of the Christian faith. Here is the validation of everything that Jesus ever did and said. We can place our faith in Him because of the empty tomb. He is Lord. He is risen. Believe in Him, trust Him, obey Him, follow Him.

> *Crown Him with many crowns.*
> *The Lamb upon His throne!*
> *Hark how the heavenly anthem drowns*
> *All music but its own!*
> *Awake my soul and sing*
> *Of Him who died for thee*
> *And hail Him as thy matchless King*
> *thro' all eternity.*
>
> *Matthew Bridges.*

When fair and open minded people consider the crucifixion and resurrection of Christ, it has a profound and lasting effect. They find themselves in this story. It becomes their story. His death becomes not some dry history but a living story that Christians for centuries have called the gospel, the good news of Jesus. His death, burial and resurrection become for us a template that explains our experience of faith. We die to sin, are buried with Him in baptism, and rise to walk in a new life, born again.

Epilogue

JESUS the crucified One, became Jesus the risen One. The Jews thought they had eliminated Him when He was nailed to the cross. The Pharisees thought they had silenced Him when they spoke against His release and called for His execution. The Romans thought they had buried Him when they placed a guard on His tomb. But somehow the corpse of Jesus just refused to lie still.

The purpose of this short book is not to prove anything beyond all doubt. The purpose is to challenge you to think about Jesus and perhaps give some consideration to Him. Many have dismissed Jesus without examining the evidence.

On September 20–23, 1976, on the campus of North Texas State University in Denton, Texas a public debate was scheduled to debate a vital issue. The protagonists were Dr Anthony Flew, Professor of Philosophy in the University of Reading, England and Dr Thomas Warren, Professor of Philosophy of Religion and Apologetics at Harding Graduate School of Religion, Memphis, Tennessee.

Dr Flew was educated at the University of Oxford, serving in RAF Intelligence in the latter part of World War II. He resumed his education after the war winning the prestigious John Lock Scholarship in Mental Philosophy in 1948. He held posts in philosophy at Oxford, Aberdeen, Keele, Calgary and the State University of New York. He authored several books on philosophy. In the debate Dr Flew affirmed, "I know that God does not exist." In doing so he championed the cause of atheism.

Dr Warren graduated from Abilene Christian University, gaining an M.A. degree from the University of Houston, and M.A. and Ph.D. degrees from Vanderbilt University. He has served on the faculty of

Abilene Christian University, Fort Worth Christian College (serving as both chairman of the Bible Department and President), Freed Hardeman College, and Harding Graduate School of Religion. He has authored more than 20 books including one entitled, "*Have Atheists Proved There Is No God?*" In the debate Dr Warren affirmed, "I know that God does exist." In doing so he championed the case for the Christianity.

The debate was well attended with between five thousand and seven thousand attending each evening to listen to the arguments put forward by both speakers. The book recounting the presentations of both men was published in 1977 by the National Christian Press, under the title, The Warren-Flew Debate. Though Professor Flew was a very accomplished scholar, and understood a great deal about the atheistic position, the verdict on the debate from the vast majority who heard it or read about it is that he was ill prepared for the strength of arguments presented by Professor Warren.

Among the powerful arguments that Professor Warren presented were...

- Either matter is eternal or the eternal God created it.
- Life must have sprung from that which is not life spontaneously.
- Consciousness has sprung from that which has no consciousness.
- Intelligence must have come from that which had no intelligence.
- Human beings must have arisen from that which was not human.
- Human beings must have arisen consequently from rocks and dirt, or from a Creator.
- Morality has evolved from that which is amoral if there is no God. Dr Warren used the example of the holocaust and asked the question if we can know that it was wrong. If we agree it is wrong, then by what law is it wrong? It was not wrong according to the German law pertaining at that time, and those people were not under the law of the United Kingdom. The closing address at the Nuremberg Trials said that they appealed to a higher law (the law of God) rather than the provincial and transient. God has placed within each one of us a sense of right and wrong which would declare this to be wrong, universally and eternally wrong.

So comprehensive, and unanswered were Dr Warren's arguments that National Christian Press thought to publish the debate as it was felt that it contributed to the arguments for faith rather than faithlessness.

Further we note that in 2007, some thirty years later, Professor Flew published another, and his final book, which was entitled, "There Is A God". The champion of the atheistic cause had totally reversed his point of view. In this interesting little book, published by HarperOne, Professor Flew tells us that the underlying principle of all of his work was to follow the evidence wherever it led. He tells us that after a lifetime of considering these issues he now has to reverse his position and admit that a sound philosophy demands that there is indeed a God. The book splits into two main sections. "Part I : My Denial of the Divine" and "Part II: My Discovery of the Divine."

Amongst the quotes from significant people in the field at the beginning of the book is the following from Daniel N. Robinson, Philosophy Department, Oxford University.

> "In *There Is A God,* one of the leading analytical philosophers of the twentieth century shares with readers an intellectual pilgrimage that begins with healthy and principled scepticism and culminates in a theism based on rational warrants and a willingness to follow the evidence as given".

Follow the evidence!

That was the basis on which such a complete reversal resulted in the mind of Anthony Flew. When he examined and kept on examining the evidence he was compelled to change his position and declare with a praiseworthy honesty— I now know there is a God.

Follow the evidence!

What about Jesus? Eye witness testimony has been recorded and preserved from antiquity. The richness of the manuscript evidence, thousands of manuscripts or parts of manuscripts. gives us a degree of confidence that we are indeed reading the accounts written in ancient times by eye witnesses. These apostles gave their lives rather than change this testimony concerning amazing Jesus of Nazareth.

My hope is that you have enjoyed reading this short book about Amazing Jesus and that it has whetted your appetite to make a more considered approach to following the evidence.

There is something about this Jesus. Would you like to know more? We can help you with a home based reflective reading of the gospel story, either by correspondence or with the help of a personal tutor or guide. If you are in Dundee we would encourage you to come and visit our services on Sundays or perhaps join a house group study to learn more. We always have a number of visitors to these meetings and coming along is not making a pledge, just coming along to see what this Jesus person is all about, what Christianity is all about.

Please see the contact details on the next page, and feel free to contact me if you want to ask specific questions about what I have written. If you are not in the Dundee area, you may find that local contacts will have been inserted on this page that you can follow up. If not please contact me and I will send you contact details for your area.

I appreciate your willingness to read through this book and consider or even.... Follow the evidence!!

Dundee Area (U.K.) contact details:
Worship Services Dundee Church of Christ:
Barnhill Community Centre/Church of Christ,
1 Campfield Square,
Broughty Ferry,
Dundee DD5 2PU

Sundays: 10:15 Bible Study meeting.
                11:15 Worship

House Groups and study groups in various locations at different times in the week, contact me for details.

Alastair's email address: doctoral@sky.com

Or write to me marking it for my personal attention at the above address, if you would like to ask any question or request a home based reflective reading course with a tutor or by correspondence.

If you come from some other part of the UK, or even some other part of the world I would hope to be able to put you in touch with someone in your area who can help you to get to know the Amazing Jesus of the Gospel story. My prayers go with you on your journey of faith.